Using Batteries

Chris Oxlade

Heinemann Library
Chicago, Illinois

www.capstonepub.com
Visit our website to find out
more information about
Heinemann-Raintree books.

To order:
☎ Phone 888-454-2279
💻 Visit www.capstonepub.com
to browse our catalog and order online.

Edited by Daniel Nunn, Rebecca Rissman, and Catherine Veitch
Designed by Joanna Hinton-Malivoire
Picture research by Elizabeth Alexander
Production by Eirian Griffiths
Originated by Capstone Global Library, Ltd.
Printed and bound in China by Leo Paper Products Ltd

16 15 14
10 9 8 7 6 5 4 3 2

Library of Congress Cataloging-in-Publication Data
Oxlade, Chris.
 Using batteries / Chris Oxlade.
   p. cm.—(It's electric!)
 Includes bibliographical references and index.
 ISBN 978-1-4329-5675-2 (hb)—ISBN 978-1-4329-5680-6
(pb) 1. Electric batteries—Juvenile literature. I. Title.
TK2901.O95 2012
621.31'242—dc23   2011016535

Acknowledgments
The author and publisher are grateful to the following
for permission to reproduce photographs: Alamy p. 19
(© David Burton); © Capstone Global Library p. 13 (Lord
and Leverett); © Capstone Publishers pp. 4 (Karon Dubke),
5 (Karon Dubke), 6 (Karon Dubke), 8 (Karon Dubke), 10
(Karon Dubke), 11 (Karon Dubke), 12 (Karon Dubke), 14
(Karon Dubke), 16 (Karon Dubke), 18 (Karon Dubke), 21
(Karon Dubke), 23 (Karon Dubke); Corbis p. 20 (© Lester V.
Bergman); Getty Images p. 7 (Pm Images); iStockphoto
pp. 24 (© Joe Belanger), 26 (© Mlenny Photography);
NASA p. 27; Photolibrary p. 29 (Lineair/ Ton Koene);
Shutterstock pp. 15 (© Zeljko Radojko), 17 (© Nicemonkey),
22 (© Kletr), 25 (© Fedor Selivanov), 28 (© Albert Lozano).

Cover photograph of a girl reading under blanket with a
flashlight reproduced with permission of Getty Images
(Rubberball/Mark Andersen). Design background feature
reproduced with permission of Shutterstock (© silver tiger).

The publisher would like to thank John Pucek for his
assistance in the preparation of this book.

Contents

Some words are shown in bold, **like this**. You can find them in the glossary on page 30.

Using Batteries

Electricity is one of our most useful **resources**. It powers all sorts of machines from flashlights to electric cars. A **battery** is a store of electricity.

Batteries come in all sorts of shapes and sizes.

Batteries power this teddy bear to make it move.

Batteries work machines that we carry around with us. Using batteries means we don't have to connect the machines to the household electricity supply.

Electricity and Batteries

batteries

The energy in these batteries will make the flashlight work.

Electricity makes things work. It makes lights glow, it makes electric motors spin, and it makes **buzzers** buzz. Electricity is a type of energy.

A **battery** contains special materials. These materials contain energy. When a battery is connected to a machine, the energy in the materials is turned into electricity.

The energy from the batteries in a bicycle light is turned into light.

Batteries in Circuits

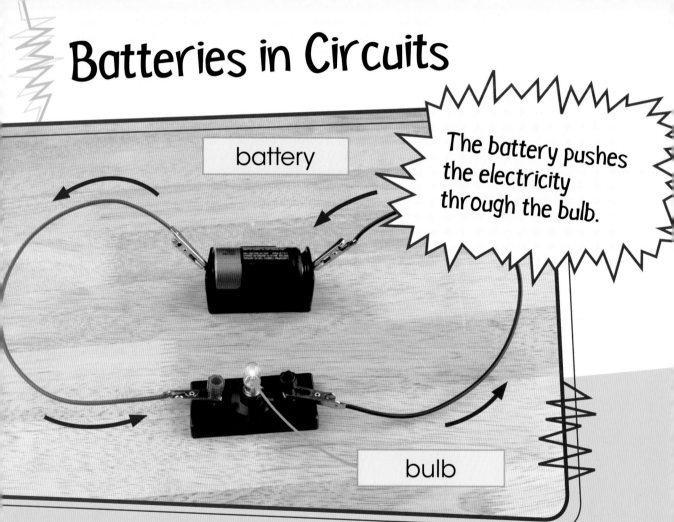

battery

The battery pushes the electricity through the bulb.

bulb

Electricity can only flow around a complete loop. The loop is called an electric **circuit**. Electricity does not flow around a circuit on its own. It needs a push. That is the job of a **battery**.

If you want to show somebody how to make an electric circuit, you can draw a picture of the circuit. This picture is called a **circuit diagram**. Small pictures called symbols show the parts of the circuit.

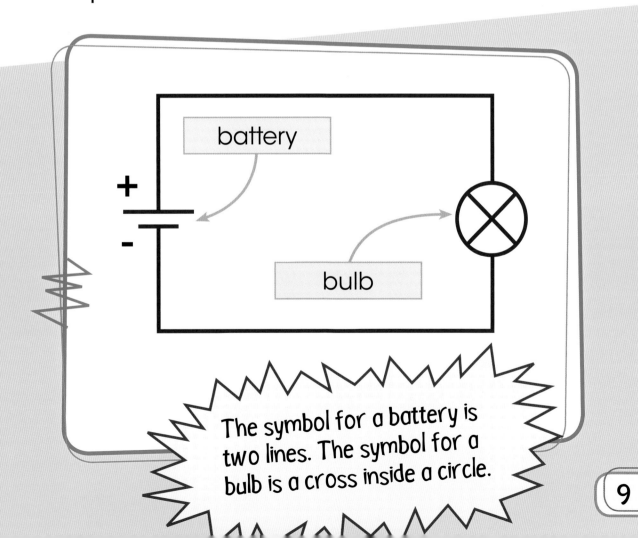

battery

bulb

The symbol for a battery is two lines. The symbol for a bulb is a cross inside a circle.

Plus and Minus

All **batteries** have two places where they join, or connect to an electric **circuit**. These places are called **terminals**. One is labeled with a "+" sign and one is labeled with a "-" sign. These labels mean plus and minus.

You can see the "+" and "-" labels on the battery in this clock.

DRY BATTERY 1.5V
R6P SIZE AA
MITSUBISHI ELECTRIC HOME APPLIANCE CO., LTD.
MADE IN CHINA

Electricity flows out of the "+" terminal. It flows back in at the "-" terminal. When you put a battery into a machine, the battery should face the right way. Otherwise the machine won't work.

Battery compartments have symbols to show you which way to put in the batteries.

Battery Shapes and Sizes

Tiny batteries like these are known as button cells.

Batteries come in all sorts of shapes and sizes. There are batteries as small as a pea. They power things such as watches and **hearing aids**. There are also batteries bigger and heavier than bricks.

There are standard battery sizes. This is so you can easily buy new batteries to replace old ones. But some things have specially shaped batteries. These batteries won't fit in other machines.

These battery sizes are D, C, AA, and 9-volt.

Batteries

This battery is a 6-volt battery.

Batteries always have some numbers and letters written on them. For example, AA batteries have 1.5 V written on them. This number shows the battery's **voltage**. Voltage tells you how much push the battery will give the electricity.

Large batteries normally have more energy in them than small batteries. A large battery will light a flashlight bulb for longer than a small battery. We often use batteries together to give electricity a bigger push.

A car battery has enough energy to make a car's engine start.

Standard and Rechargeable Batteries

standard battery

rechargeable battery

All **batteries** slowly run out of electricity as we use them. When they have completely run out, they cannot push electricity anymore. When standard batteries have run out, you cannot use them again. Then you should **recycle** them.

When some batteries run out, we can refill them with electricity. These batteries are called **rechargeable** batteries. Filling them up with electricity is called recharging. They can be recharged hundreds of times.

Symbols such as this show how much energy is left in a phone's rechargeable battery.

Recharging Batteries

To recharge a **rechargeable battery** you have to put it into a battery charger. A battery charger sends electricity into the battery. This replaces the energy in the materials inside the battery.

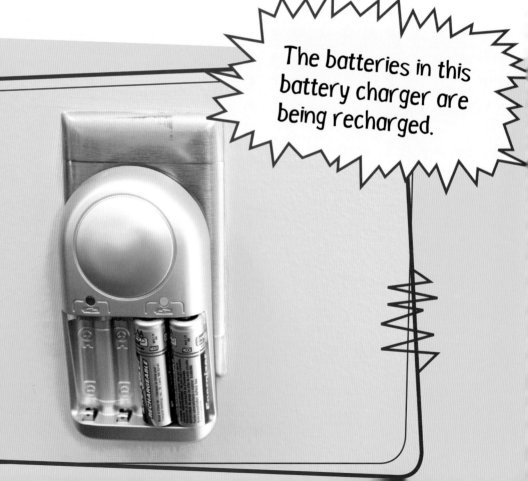

The batteries in this battery charger are being recharged.

Standard batteries cannot be recharged. You should never put standard batteries into a battery charger. It could be dangerous because harmful chemicals could leak from the batteries.

A solar battery charger uses the energy in sunshine to charge batteries.

Battery Materials

Batteries are made of many different materials. The materials inside a battery make electricity flow when the battery is connected to a **circuit**. Batteries are named after the materials inside.

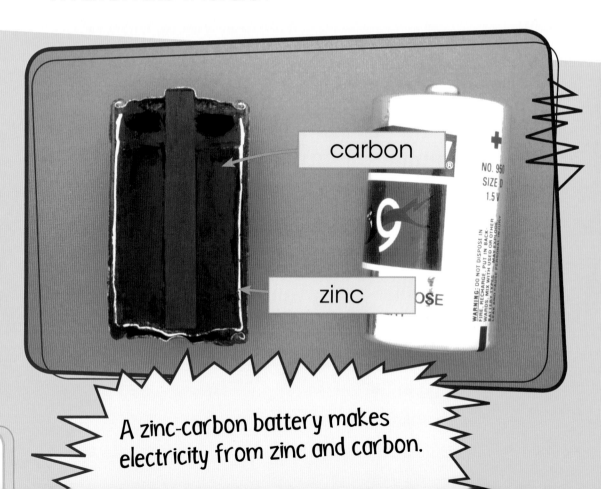

carbon

zinc

A zinc-carbon battery makes electricity from zinc and carbon.

Rechargeable batteries also contain materials that make electricity flow. A Ni-Cad battery contains nickel and cadmium. An NiMH battery contains nickel and other metals.

This camera gets its power from a lithium-ion battery.

Portable Power

This model helicopter gets its power from Ni-Cad batteries.

Cell phones, music players, and laptop computers all get their electricity from **batteries**. This means we can take them where we like. Model cars and planes also use batteries to work their motors.

battery

A cordless drill has a big **rechargeable** battery.

Many electric power tools, such as drills, saws, and screwdrivers, get their electricity from batteries. These tools are known as cordless tools because they have no power cord.

Batteries in Cars

A car has a big, powerful **battery**. The battery is needed to start the car. It works the car's electric starter motor, which starts up the engine. The battery **recharges** when the engine is going.

A car battery is heavy because it contains lots of a metal called lead.

Electric cars are pushed along by an electric motor. They don't have an engine. An electric car has lots of powerful batteries. After the car has been driven for a few hours the batteries have to be recharged.

This electric car is plugged into a recharging station.

Remote Batteries

Batteries are useful in homes where there is no electricity from a power station. These places include farms and villages in faraway areas of the world. The batteries store electricity for working lights, radios, and other machines.

wind turbine

This home has a wind turbine that recharges its batteries.

Satellites and space probes travel far from any electricity supply. They have **batteries** that power their electric **circuits**. The batteries are **recharged** by electricity from **solar cells**.

This battery-powered robot vehicle was sent to the planet Mars!

Battery Safety

Powerful **electricity** is dangerous. It can give you an electric shock, and could hurt you very badly. Even a car **battery** can give you an electric shock. Some of the materials inside batteries are harmful, so you should never cut open a battery.

Never touch a car battery. Adults should always follow instructions when handling batteries.

Some of the materials inside batteries are harmful to the environment. You should always take old batteries to your local recycling center. Then the materials inside can be **recycled**.

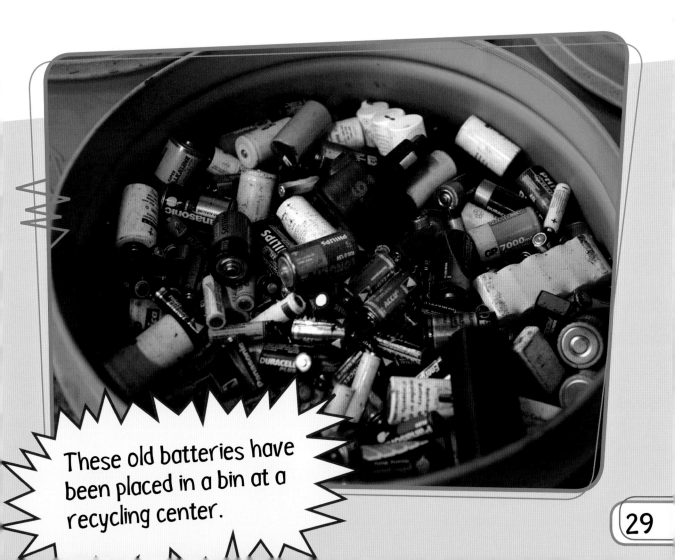

These old batteries have been placed in a bin at a recycling center.

Glossary

battery part that pushes electricity around a circuit

buzzer part that makes a buzzing sound when electricity flows through it

circuit loop that electricity flows around

circuit diagram diagram that shows how the parts in a circuit are connected

hearing aid device that goes in a person's ear and makes sound louder

rechargeable battery that can have electricity put back into it, so it can be used again

recycle use materials in an object again

resource something that we use for making things and living our lives

solar cell device that gives out electricity when light shines on it

terminal part where a component connects to a circuit

voltage size of the push that a battery gives electricity in a circuit

Find Out More

Books

Flaherty, Michael. *Electricity and Batteries (Science Factory)*. New York: Rosen, 2008.

Oxlade, Chris. *Electricity (Investigate)*. Chicago: Heinemann Raintree, 2008.

Royston, Angela. *Using Electricity (My World of Science)*. Chicago: Heinemann Raintree, 2008.

Websites

http://pbskids.org/zoom/activities/sci/lemonbattery.html
Visit this website to learn how to use a lemon as a battery.

www.andythelwell.com/blobz/
Lots of electricity activities, games, and puzzles.

www.eia.gov/kids/energy.cfm?page=electricity_home-basics-k.cfm
Learn more about electricity from this website.

Index